ESSE ★ BRIAN PINKNEY

The STONE LAMP

Eight Stories of Hanukkah Through History

HYPERION BOOKS FOR CHILDREN

NEW YORK

ACKNOWLEDGMENTS

For shining their light upon this work I gratefully acknowledge
Rabbi Noah Kitty; Randy, Kate, and Rachel Hesse; Eileen
Christelow; Robert and Tink MacLean; Liza Ketchum;
Wendy Watson; Professor Lawrence Schiffman; Uri Hurwitz;
Johanna Hurwitz; Cantor Alvin Donald; Geraldine Donald;
Jonathan Ray; and Donna Bray.

—K.H.

For information address Hyperion Books for Children, 114 Fifth Avenue, New York, New York 10011-5690.
1 3 5 7 9 10 8 6 4 2
Printed in Singapore
Library of Congress Cataloging-in-Publication Data on file.
ISBN 0-7868-0619-2 (trade ed.)
ISBN 0-7868-2531-6 (lib. ed.)

Visit www.hyperionchildrensbooks.com

To Rabbi Noah Kitty

—K.H.

For Donna Bray and Anne Diebel

—B.P.

In 164 B.C.E., Jewish rebel fighters under the command of Judah Maccabee defeated the Syrian general Lysias and entered Jerusalem. Reclaiming the Holy Temple, Judah had the defiled altar demolished and a new one built. When the work was completed, the Temple was rededicated with a celebratory festival lasting eight days.

So Hanukkah, the midwinter festival of lights, began.

The Crusades

Until Richard the Lion Heart came to power, England did not fight in the Crusades. (The Crusades, a series of religious wars that began in the eleventh century, were waged by European Christians to regain Jerusalem from the Muslims.) But King Richard's enthusiasm for battle brought England forward, in 1189, to lead the Third Crusade. Muslims were the primary target of Crusaders making their way toward Palestine. Jews along the route and in England suffered as well.

The Jews of York, in the north of England, heard rumors from other villages about unrestrained Crusaders. At first they dismissed these stories. But on March 16, 1190, a crusading mob stormed the Jewish quarter of York. Many Jews died in their homes or in the bloody chaos that spilled into the streets that day, but some escaped.

One group of 150 sought protection in Clifford's Tower, a wooden castle on the southern edge of York. A local sheriff ushered the fleeing Jews inside the castle, but could not defend them against the frenzied mob. As Crusaders stormed the tower with lit torches, the trapped Jews weighed the ultimatum of conversion or death. They chose death, cheating the flames by taking their own lives before the fire reached them.

First Night, First Light

YORK, ENGLAND, 1190

I rock Aaron in his cradle,
the sheepskin, soft with years,
falls and rises gently with his breath.
Elijah, the cat, brushes against the table leg
and Mother grinds the green cheese
for tonight's tarts.

Aaron wakes as Mother rolls the crust.
His plump hand waves in the air and he jabbers,
crowing as the tip of Elijah's ginger tail
tickles his palm.
I chop the bulbous onions,
shedding strong tears, my nose running.

3

Father always had a cloth ready.
I remember once I came upon him in the field behind our house.
I thought him dead, so deeply he slept in the cradle of the spring sun.
Kneeling, rooted in quiet grief, I woke him,
my round tears tickling the lids of his dark eyes.
How gently he dried my tears then.

Now he is gone.
Yet our rooms still fill with the smell of onions and cloves
and Aaron bounces in my lap.
My cousins tumble in.
Mother wags a finger at Reuben as he reaches for a hot tart, and Leah
chases Elijah around the cradle, making Aaron laugh deep in his belly.

After the meal we light the first light in our lamp of stone.
Mother touches the flame to the wick. We are thick with tart and thankful,
for though we have lost much,
yet this much remains. I hold Aaron,
crumbs clinging to his moist chin,
I hold my brother up in the glow of the Hanukkah light,
and the flame dances
in Aaron's dark eyes.

Tamara, age 10, escaped with her mother, her aunt, and her cousins to an appointed hiding place. Her father and uncle were among those who perished at Clifford's Tower.

The Burning of the Books

Nicholas Donin was born a Jew. He studied under Rabbi Yehiel, the most respected Jewish leader in thirteenth-century Paris. When that same rabbi cut Donin off from the Jewish community for his heretical views, the former student lashed out. Donin railed against Judaism, declaring passages from the Talmud (the collection of writings constituting Jewish civil and religious law) to be blasphemous. He sent inflammatory letters to Pope Gregory IX. In response, the pope called for a series of public disputations, requiring Jewish scholars to defend their teachings. Nothing fair or honorable came to light in these "debates." They were little more than fixed trials staged to condemn Judaism.

Following the disputations, the pope ordered the confiscation and destruction of all the offending books. From the lessons of the sages to the commentaries of Rashi (an important eleventh-century French rabbi), these pre-Gutenberg manuscripts were irreplaceable. The revered volumes, housed in the private libraries of Paris, filled twenty-four open wagons . . . thousands and thousands of treasured, handwritten tomes.

The public executioner arrived in June 1242 in the Place de Grève, under the shadow of Notre Dame, and with great ceremony burned every page of Hebraic learning collected in Paris.

Second Night, Second Light

In the morning, I sit on the rough hearth rug,
leaning against Papa's legs.
All the boys gather round for warmth,
staring at the shelf where Papa's books once stood.
Papa rests on his stool and pokes the embers, and for a moment
I am rising with the sparks into the Paris sky.

In the afternoon my sister sends me for firewood. On my way
I read the butcher's face, red and fleshy,
with the same streak of white in his hair as his father;
I read the musky squirrel pelts, hanging in the marketplace,
not one color at all, but four: white and gray, black and brown;
I read the windows of Notre Dame.

I read the quick movements of the hat maker
and the hand signs of the waterman as he directs boats up and down the Seine;
I read the glint of wet stones on the riverbank,
and the bark of trees crowning under a painted sky;
I read the gentle rub of the spinning wheel, the sigh of its pedal,
and the loom hushing the weaver's complaints with its rushing shuttle;
I read the bent figure of my grandfather, as he reaches to help me with my load of sticks;
and I read Mama's face, steeped in a thousand thoughts, stirred to a smile.

Tonight,
in our warm room,
in the heart of Paris, under a star-washed sky,
Papa lights the wicks of our stone Hanukkah lamp,
given him years ago in exchange for a kindness.
And while the lamp burns,
Papa opens his arms like a great book.
He takes me into his lap
and whispers in my ear
the words of Rashi.

Jeremie, age 8, balanced on a windowsill overlooking the Place de Grève, witnessed the burning of the books.

The Inquisition

Between the thirteenth and sixteenth centuries, many Jews from Spain and Portugal were forced to turn their backs on their religion and accept Christianity. These Jews were called *conversos*. Adopting Christianity often offered Jews their only hope of avoiding persecution, of holding on to property, and of staying alive. Some of these conversos truly adopted the Christian faith, but many made only outward concessions to Christianity, remaining observant Jews in the privacy of their homes and the privacy of their hearts. The Church blamed these "secret" Jews for corrupting true Christians and condemned many of them to death by fire.

A wealthy woman of Portuguese birth named Gracia Nasi defied the authorities of the Inquisition. She possessed power, intelligence, and wealth, and she used her influence to help others escape persecution and death. Denounced as a secret Jew by her sister-in-law, Gracia spent time imprisoned. Her release came only after Joseph, her nephew, arranged diplomatic intervention. Daringly, Gracia Nasi continued her humanitarian acts even after her release. She eventually settled in Turkey, where the sultan's more tolerant attitude permitted conversos to practice Judaism openly.

Third Night, Third Light

VENICE, ITALY, 1546

Joseph stays at my side tonight,
his kind eyes anchoring me on the low bench.
Our fingers nearly touch.

He laughs softly and says,
Reyna, you are dreaming with your eyes open,
and I tell him I am not dreaming,
only remembering the time I danced with the girls
in Belgium, arms laced,
our circle of voices rising from the hill of wild strawberries,
the sun warming our hair through our scarves.

Mother makes ready the lamp,
though she dares not place it in the tall window.
The stone lamp is not our most beautiful.
But it is our oldest and dearest, a present from Uncle Diogo,
dear Uncle Diogo, who always smelled of honeyed lemons.

Joseph slices an apple with his knife.
Mother takes her share daintily, holding each small bite in her mouth.
I am too impetuous, my piece does not last long.
Joseph eats like a man.
He smiles around the white flesh as he chews,
and I think of the sweet taste in each of our mouths,
and our lips moving like friends sharing a secret.

Outside, the call of geese.
I glimpse a flutter of white
and for a moment I see
        angels gliding past our window,
            the light from our room glazing their wings.

I rise to my feet, press my face to the glass.
Joseph comes close behind me and Mother behind him.
Her shadow cloaks us
        and the wings of the geese
            fall soft as veils across our faces.

Reyna, age 15, daughter of Gracia Nasi, later married her cousin Joseph, and together the two continued Gracia Nasi's humanitarian work.

The False Messiah

In 1626, in the Turkish city of Smyrna, a Jewish family welcomed the birth of their newest son. As the boy matured, his extraordinary scholarship gained recognition. So, too, grew his reputation for extreme behavior. During bouts of depression, he fought with demons. During euphoric moments, he spoke and behaved as a man touched by the finger of God. In 1665, during one of those euphoric states, Shabbatai Zevi (pronounced SHAH-bah-tie ZVEE) proclaimed himself the Messiah. In large part because of the active endorsement of Nathan of Gaza, nearly the entire Diaspora (Jews scattered throughout Europe and the Middle East), from the working classes to the wealthiest members, embraced Shabbatai Zevi as the redeemer and Messiah. Jews sold their homes, abandoned their shops, and neglected their fields with the expectation of following Shabbatai Zevi to the Holy Land.

Before the appointed day for departure, however, the Turkish sultan, perceiving Shabbatai Zevi as a threat, placed him under arrest. In the sultan's custody, Shabbatai Zevi was given a choice between execution and conversion. He chose to save his own life, casting off his Judaism and adopting instead the ways of a Muslim. Worldwide, Jews descended into despair.

Fourth Night, Fourth Light

SMYRNA, TURKEY, 1666

I sit on the doorstep in the twilight,
shivering, lighting wicks that
cannot quicken our crushed hearts.
I cover my head with my hood and
wrap my arms around my knees.
The dull tooth of winter gnaws through my thin boots,
my threadbare skirt—
all I have left after giving away my best.

Today, I fetched water from the well, chopped onions,
ground herbs, and fried potatoes in searing oil.
But this evening, again, no one stops
to share our table or our shattered dreams.
The night everywhere silent and brooding.

My little brother slips out first to join me.
He tucks his small hands under my arm.
My sister comes next, close against me.
Then Grandmother and Mother,
then Father and my older brother.
We huddle together on the doorstep
behind the stone lamp as,
one by one, Hanukkah lights ignite,
        flickering silver at the top of the hill,
        silver in the hollow,
        silver along the edges of the field.
    Buoyant, my sister rises to sing
and we join her, our voices ornamenting the darkness.
    In answer,
        from the top of the hill,
        from the hollow,
        from the edges of the field,
        a chorus of voices swells to meet ours

and we remember. We are not alone.

Havva, age 16, grew up in Odemis, not far from the birthplace of Shabbatai Zevi. She gave away her good boots and her best clothes in anticipation of following the Messiah to the Holy Land.

The Pogroms

In Russia, from the late nineteenth to the early twentieth century, Jews suffered through a succession of organized massacres (pogroms). The first of these assaults occurred from 1881 to 1884 after Czar Alexander II's assassination. Russians were vengeful, hungry for vindication, blaming the Jews for the czar's death. They struck at Jews with brutal attacks.

These pogroms sent a host of Jews fleeing their homes, seeking safety, freedom, and tolerance in Germany, and later in North and South America. The perilous conditions in Europe and Russia also gave rise to the Zionist movement, as Jews resolved to leave behind such persecutions and resettle where they hoped at last to be safe—in their ancestral homeland: Palestine.

Fifth Night, Fifth Light

KIEV, UKRAINE, 1883

Papa was bringing his beets,
his sweet sugar beets to market.
The day so blue,
the path dappled under a soft mantle of sunlight.
Papa was bringing his beets in the waning days of summer
and I did not go.
I walked instead, barefoot through the tall grass.
I rested, satisfied, in the shadow of trees.

19

Now, in the bitter days of winter, I
bring the sweet beets to sell,
digging them from the root cellar.
I tie my kerchief over my ears, and stride, proud-backed, rough-booted,
across the snow, my brother with his sack,
I with my patched basket. We stop at each hut,
and I trade for crusty bread, pickled fish, lamp wicks.
Dany keeps his eyes down, but I lift my chin and set my smile
and reach out my bare hand to receive what is offered.

Papa will not plant beets again,
nor light the wicks in the ancient lamp,
        the stone lamp given *his* papa in trade for beets.
We light the lamp for Papa,
on the wooden step, defiant,
        though the mob may come again to finish what it started.
Mother lifts Papa to see what he no longer understands,
while my brother Micha
counts our money, promising *Next year in Jerusalem,*
and my brother Dany slips away,
to join a revolution.

*Anichka, age 13, nursed her brutally beaten father after the pogrom of 1883. He never recovered
from his injuries.*

Kristallnacht

In November 1938, the assassination of a German diplomat at the hands of a distressed Jew gave Nazi hatred a long-awaited signal to explode. Hitler had been chancellor of Germany for five years when Kristallnacht (the Night of Broken Glass) shattered the lives of European Jewry and jolted the machinery of the Holocaust into motion.

That night, across Germany and Austria, anti-Semitic rage splintered and roared with the destruction of Jewish homes, shops, warehouses, and synagogues. At least 30,000 Jewish citizens from Germany and Austria (Jewish intellectuals, in particular) were ordered aboard trains bound for concentration camps.

Government edicts against Jews enacted as early as 1933 reached new restrictive heights. These laws hampered Jewish businesses and denied professionals the freedom to practice. Jews, severed from society, were barred from attending public events or participating in cultural activities. Jewish children could not attend public schools.

The Jews did not entirely surrender to this outrage. Some sought safety in other countries. Others who remained in Europe led uprisings, revolts, and resistance movements. But the balance of power shifted too heavily against the Jews. The light of the Jewish people, overwhelmed by unspeakable acts of hatred, was nearly extinguished in Hitler's "Final Solution" to the "Jewish problem."

Sixth Night, Sixth Light

GRAZ, AUSTRIA, 1938

The snow falls, fat flakes,
clinging to rooftops, carpeting sidewalks.
I head quickly home to beat the curfew for Jews,
an invisible boy, moving through the streets of Graz.
As soon as I come through the door
the smell of fried potato pancakes leaps to my nose
and carves a hole in my stomach.
Mama stands in the kitchen doorway,
the white platter piled high with latkes,
    though it is only the three of us now.
At the table my sister Lucie sits.
Her hands rest on one of Papa's books—
    how did she move it off the high shelf,
    she is so small, the book so big?

23

I help Mama set the table.
Lucie insists we leave the book at Papa's seat where she placed it.
We eat latkes, their edges crisp and brown,
spooning onto our plates sour cream and applesauce.
We spin the dreidel and Lucie climbs into my lap.
I stroke her hair and tell her how
      once we built a snowman
      wrapping it in Papa's blue scarf
      using lumps of coal for its eyes.
Lucie pleads for us to build a snowman now.
I tell her no.
I tell her the snow that falls in Graz is too dirty,
but she can see for herself the white truth outside our windows.
My sister's unyielding face moves me. Silently, I dress her in her coat and mittens.
Silently, bundled against the sharp wind,
she and I build a snowman in the yard.
Mama's solemn smile floats above the golden lights in the Hanukkah lamp.

Later that night, so much later, as Lucie turns and sighs contentedly in her sleep,
Mama and I carefully unmake the snowman, smoothing the yard,
certain even this small joy is forbidden to Jews.
We hang the blue scarf tenderly back on the peg, place the coal eyes in the stove,
and warm our hands around cups of sweet tea.

David, age 11, hid in a wardrobe with his mother and sister as his father and brothers were rounded up on Kristallnacht.

Exodus 1947

So many more lives could have been plucked from the finality of the gas chambers, from the horrors of the camps, so much suffering could have been prevented if the free world had opened its doors. Instead, quietly, with pitifully few exceptions, governments blocked Jewish immigration throughout those terrible years.

After the war ended, Jewish refugees sought surviving family members; they searched for a way to begin living again. Many of these survivors chose to start over in Palestine, a British territory. But the British, under Arab pressure, found ways of keeping the Jews out. Ships crowded with refugees were turned away from Palestine's borders. Barely seaworthy, these vessels sometimes sank in their pursuit of a safe harbor, either accidentally or as a result of aggressive British measures.

In 1947, the *Exodus*, a converted ferry, made its bid for Palestine, carrying nearly 5,000 Jewish refugees, including 1,000 orphans. These exhausted men, women, and children endured life aboard the cramped ship with dignity, despite the overwhelming heat, inadequate facilities, and insufficient food. They refused to surrender to assaults by the British, fighting back with tin cans and raw potatoes, the only weapons they had. The world watched as the British turned these Jews away from Palestine, and forcibly unloaded them at a detention center in Hamburg, Germany.

Seventh Night, Seventh Light

HAMBURG, GERMANY, 1947

We fading embers, we tired remnants of the *Exodus*
gather around the stone Hanukkah lamp.
No one knows how it came to be here or why.
But we find oil and wicks and set the lamp ablaze
against the German night.

From the edge of the clearing I watch:

A girl of fourteen and a man in his twenties
sit at a stump and spin a hand-carved dreidel.
A mother leans against the wind, holding her child,
who is four, though she looks barely two.
Their cold cheeks press, side by side,
their arms circle
each around the other
in soft curves. Eyes lowered,
their dark lashes rest on their cheeks.

27

An older man with a beard steadies his large hands
on the shoulders of a girl in a purple coat.
She looks warm and content in the middle of the fenced yard.
There are three who go everywhere together, two boys and a girl.
One boy is the girl's brother, the other her love.
I knew them on the ship.

Leaning against the fence, I see

      soldiers prowling like wolves,
        moving with their guns poised, their hats cocked, their hatred
        casting shadows across the camp.

But there are no soldiers now,
only ghosts.
I must remember.
It is the baby in her mother's arms that is real,
the girl in the purple coat,
and the stone menorah,
radiant in the snowy yard,
shining against the German night.

Mathe, age 16, one of the children on Exodus 1947, *thought he had lost all his family at Buchenwald.*
When he finally reached Jerusalem, he was reunited with a cousin and two aunts.

Assassination of Rabin

From the time they began reclaiming Palestine as their homeland in the late 1800s, Jews encountered anger, resistance, and attacks. From without: the aggression of neighboring countries and British authorities. From within: the outrage of uncompromising radical Jews, and the displaced citizens of Palestine.

Arab extremists, with violent acts of terrorism, were determined to drive Jews away. At the same time, Jewish extremists, blinded by fanaticism, sabotaged Israel's overtures of reconciliation with its Arab neighbors and the uprooted Palestinians. This resistance by Jewish radicals exploded in November 1995 when a law student assassinated Prime Minister Yitzhak Rabin at a gathering where representatives from Egypt, Jordan, and Morocco stood beside Rabin on an elevated stage, united in the common cause of peace.

Eighth Night, Eighth Light

TEL AVIV, ISRAEL, 1995

Abba bends his long legs
and curves his back to light our Hanukkah lamp.
Outside, the city sparkles, every window a shining jewel.
A dove perches on the sill and looks back into our flat
with the red-and-gold curtains and the long sofa
with its velvet pillows.
Abba sings the blessing over the lamp.
And after,
my sister, Ziva, sings "The Song of Peace,"
        the song Rabin sang before he was shot.
My sister sings the song often,
        while she and Ema pack her blue-and-white-
        striped bag for school,
        while she draws at the kitchen table
        crayon pictures of coffins flying with wings
        and clouds crying tears.

31

Ziva, her wild hair gathered in pigtails,
stands on her toes and gazes at the burning wicks,
her skinny legs bring her almost to the height of the sill,
her skinny arms spread out, half in balance, half in wonder.
Ziva, Ema, Abba, and I stand together before the stone lamp.
It has passed from one family to the next.
It is homely beside the menorahs of my friends.
But I am proud to join my hand with the many who have lighted it.

The boy who shot Rabin—
he thought he could stop something.
He was wrong.
I look at this ancient lamp and know
some things cannot be stopped.

One of those things
is the Light.

Ori, age 12, attended, with his father, the peace rally where Prime Minister Yitzhak Rabin was assassinated. Father and son remained that night, standing vigil with hundreds of others, the glow of their combined candles illuminating the Israeli night.

Sometimes, a flame can be utterly extinguished.
Sometimes, a flame can shrink and waver, but
sometimes a flame refuses to go out. It flares up from the faintest ember to
illuminate the darkness,
to burn in spite of overwhelming odds.

So burns the Light of the Jewish people.
So burn the Lights of Hanukkah.

AUTHOR'S NOTE

When first contemplating a Hanukkah book spanning centuries, I hardly knew where to begin. I pulled from my shelves piles of books on Jewish history and culture, dipping into each one. Every source succeeded in adding new considerations to a seemingly insurmountable quantity of material, ranging from which moments in Jewish history to include, to which of several variant spellings of *Hanukkah* to employ. One particular book saved this project from being snuffed out before it had a chance to ignite. Brimful of facts, *The Jewish Almanac*, compiled and edited by Richard Siegel and Carl Rheins, contained an entry titled "The People Cried." Ultimately, this entry proved indispensable in narrowing the field and directing me to the periods on which I eventually focused.

The Stone Lamp illuminates the time line of Jewish history at eight widely spaced intervals. Knowing how alien these moments in history might seem to contemporary readers, I felt it important to include not only the facts (the *Encyclopedia Judaica* supplied a wealth of information), but the homey details of everyday life that might help readers relate to a distant and unfamiliar past. *The Power of Light* by Isaac Bashevis Singer proved surprisingly helpful. For each story in Singer's book, Irene Lieblich painted a luminous illustration. That Chagall-like artwork inspired many of the details in the poetry of *The Stone Lamp*.

Many translations of the Bible passed through my hands as I searched for apt quotations to accompany each historical event. I found most useful a 1901 King James translation with an excellent concordance and word index. With the exception of the biblical passage for the fifth night (from the J.P.S. Tanakh), all quotations are from the King James.

The journeys we take often lead us down unexpected paths. The journey I took to create *The Stone Lamp* started many years ago when I was working on *A Time of Angels*. I contacted Rabbi Noah Kitty to clarify certain religious points in the novel. The rabbi was so helpful that I continued to consult with her on religious themes in my work. Soon, I found myself attending services regularly. The rabbi taught me to read the Torah. Over time, she brought me back to my religious roots, rekindling my own guttering flame. I would not have, nor could I have, written *The Stone Lamp* without the wisdom and assistance of Rabbi Kitty.

—Karen Hesse